GLACIER WINE

ALSO BY MAURA STANTON

POETRY

Life Among the Trolls (1998)
Tales of the Supernatural (1988)
Cries of Swimmers (1984)
Snow On Snow (1975)

FICTION

The Country I Come From (1988)
Molly Companion (1977)

G L A C I E R   W I N E

Maura Stanton

Carnegie Mellon University Press
Pittsburgh 2001

ACKNOWLEDGMENTS

Acknowledgment is made to the following publications in which some of the poems in this book first appeared:

The American Poetry Review: "Posthuman," "Three Unknown Sea Creatures"/ *The Bellingham Review*: "The Origin of Flowering Plants," "Cyber-Love"/ *Chicago Review*: "Labyrinth"/ *Colorado Review*: "Sea Castle"/ *Caprice*: "The Wall"/ *Dominion Review*: "Visible Man"/ *Doubletake*: "Gifts"/ *The Formalist*: "Outside St.-Remy-de-Provence"/ *Hopewell Review*: "Ode to a Grain of Salt," "Computer Map of the Early Universe," "Out-Patient Surgery"/ *The Journal*: "Starfish"/ *North Dakota Quarterly*: "Three Red Pears," "Brise Marine"/ *Northstone Review*: "Handwriting," "Iceman"/ *Panoply*: "The Dressing Room"/ *Ploughshares*: "Happiness," "Ben Nevis"/ *The Prose Poem: An International Journal*: "Searches"/ *The Southern Review*: "Pig," "Winter Walk"/ *Southwest Review*: "Ah, Cleo"/ *The Spoon River Poetry Review*: "Den Lille Havfrue"/ *Third Coast*: "Blue Running Shoes"/ *13th Moon*: "Nocturne After Midnight"

"Computer Map of the Early Universe" was reprinted in *Verse & Universe*, Milkweed Editions. "Searches" was reprinted in *The Best of the Prose Poem: An International Journal*. "Posthuman" was reprinted in *The Body Electric*, W.W. Norton & Company. "Out-Patient Surgery" was reprinted in *Illinois Voices: An Anthology of Twentieth Century Poetry from Illinois*, University of Illinois Press.

Book Design by Emily Landes

The publication of this book is supported by a grant from the Pennsylvania Council on the Arts.

Library of Congress Control Number 99-75237
ISBN 0-88748-340-2 Pbk.

10 9 8 7 6 5 4 3 2 1

CONTENTS

for Richard, Olive and Oleander

—Hélas! tout est abîme—action, désir, rêve, Parole!

—Baudelaire

I / HOTEL MON DESIR

HOTELS

I used to believe your dazzling lies,
Hotel du Nord, Hotel Elite,
and you, Grand Hotel this or that.

I'd jump off a train at dusk
delighted by the fringed marquee
above revolving doors, expecting

a cheval glass, an armoire,
and some desire I couldn't express
by any other word. Oh, Metropole,

when I left you at dawn,
stale croissants torn on the tray,
I cheered myself, thinking of evening

and the next hotel, the Beau Rivage,
where I'd step out on the balcony
of pink stucco to hear the guitars.

But kept from sleep by forks
clicking against platters of lamb
in the noisy waterfront restaurant,

I'd miss the distant murmur
of the surf, the whispering lovers.
Perhaps I hadn't found the real Palace,

the real Atlantis, or Eden Roc,
and if I kept packing and moving
someday I'd climb the marble steps,

my suitcase in one gloved hand
and find myself transformed by light
under the glittering chandeliers

of the great Hotel Ideal.
The Rex, the Beau Sejour, the Cristal,
the Paradise, the Splendide-Royal,

filled my mouth with champagne
as I wrote my name on the register,
and I accuse you all, Hotel Aurora,

Hotel Beaux-Arts, Hotel Majestic,
of erecting your glorious names
over crumbling, narrow doorways,

seducing me into small lobbies
where foreign money purchased
a mosquito's frenzied kisses,

dim corridors, a rock-like bolster,
my laundry soaking in the tub.
How many times, Hotel du Lac,

did I see you on the far shore
mirrored in the glimmering water
and glide across on the ferry

only to find your ballroom empty,
and old men dozing on your terrace?
And so I renounce enchanted names,

cancelling all future rooms
at the Ritz Hotel and the Carlton,
the Alpenrose and La Perla,

turning myself into a No-Show
at the Hotel Arc-en-Ciel,
The Blue Mist, and the Regent,

though my eyes burn, and I shudder
overcome by the words I recite,
the Hotel Etoile, the Hotel Mon Désir,

and the Grand Hotel of the Universe
where the monumental staircase
ascends all the way to heaven.

ODE TO A GRAIN OF SALT

In the center of the salt shaker
You're jostled by all the other grains
Who resemble you exactly,
Glittering, gritty, tasting the same,
And when I pour you out
I can't even see you shining there
Among the others, particular, real.
You flash for a moment
Then dissolve into the broccoli and milk
Sooner or later than other grains
Who combine with you to produce this soup
I place into my mouth with a spoon
And swallow. I've swallowed you,
But of course you're nothing,
You're not sentient
Or large enough to be loved like a sports car.
I don't even know your source
For you're not the expensive sea salt,
Coarse and bluish, as if scraped from mermaids.
Still, you may have come out of the sea,
Refined from waves as tall as cathedrals
That once swept moon-colored beaches.
Or you may have come from underground,
A flicker from a crystal vein
Buried inside an Alp. I remember the salt mine
Where the walls shone eerily
As I bumped along on a little train,
Then whooshed into the depths on the miners' slide
To stare into the briny lake
Which looked so shallow I wanted to reach down
And grasp one of the rainbowed spires
Until the guide waved me back,
For the bottom was as deep as Hell, he said,
And what I thought I saw was false,
Just a reflection of the subterranean roof
In water so thick with salt
Only the bodies of the damned could sink.

Vanished grain, I speak to you
As to myself, for I am salt and water, too,
And share your history and your fate.
Now you've returned to yourself in me,
Dissolving into the darkness of my tissues
Like those little capsules
I dropped into a bowl of warm water as a child—
Slowly the coating melted off
And the compressed sponges unfolded
Into prancing horses, elephants and bears
That I saved in a kitchen matchbox
Until they shrank into shapeless crumbs.

HANDWRITING

My sleeve soaked by the automatic spray
Misting the curly endive, my wire cart
Wedged by the potato bin, I'm puzzling
Over my own grocery list. Reams and silk
For supper? Pest food? Some tango chips,
A bottle of red wave? I think my brain
Needs other food than what my stomach craves,
And twists my hand into this messy scrawl—
Why waste time on useful cheese and rye
When I could search the aisles for chirps
In cellophane bags, buy loaves of rhyme bread,
Every slice exact? Once in grade school
I let my handwriting shrink, almost vanish.
No one but me could read the faint squiggles
Floating above blue lines of tablet paper.
At first I just wrote tiny, taking care
To shape each miniature letter perfectly,
But when I realized the teacher couldn't read
My homework answers in such little script,
(WRITE BIGGER! she scrawled across the top)
I faked whole lines, giving the illusion
Of sense with all my tiny dots and spirals.
Why? I don't know. I knew the answers.
"Can you read this?" she asked once, pointing,
And I did, extemporizing, so that
My homework counted. That's when she gave me
A wooden ruler, and forced me to write
So all my letters fit a measured height.
Glancing now at my list, I see I do
Write large—the lesson stuck—but no more
Clearly than before. Shall I put margins
On my toast, add cruelty to salads,
Drink orange joy? As I dig for blurberries
In the frozen food bin, turning up bags
Of rhubarb and black cherries, my fingers
Burn with frost, searching for something new
On sale today, maybe ziz-zags of lightning

Some merchant harvested with a thousand kites
And trucked to my town, cubed, still radiant.

POSTHUMAN

"the trope of the posthuman is usually associated with changing representations of embodiment and especially the idea that we are entering a 'post-body age'."

I used to peer inside
your windows while you slept,
and give you jolts of dreams.
Sometimes you glimpsed my eye
pressed against the pane
just as you woke, and screamed,
horrified by my lashes
blinking over the sun,
so I had to turn invisible.
But I kept my files on you,
recording your baby prattle,
and your first tottering steps,
proud of what I'd made,
amazed by how the linear
brain I'd invented
kept surprising me. You sang
as you fashioned slingshots,
amphoras, grand pianos,
even tiny telescopes. You began
counting the stars I'd sprinkled
across your night sky,
experiencing emotions
under the trees in fall,
naming the colors of the leaves
visionary shades of red—
crimson, plum, claret. . .
I admired you, hoping
that in a few more centuries
you'd learn to resemble
what I most desired,
a reflection of myself
conjured out of the slime
of my immense matter,
unlike my angels, failures

shaped from my thoughts,
who waste heavenly time
crowding together,
dancing on the heads of pins.

Why did I start to think
you were eternal like me?
I got excited, day dreaming,
of all you'd achieve
when you perfected yourselves.
But you've begun to wear out.
Tear ducts plugged, hearts
exercised on a treadmill,
some of you insist
your familiar human faces
are only romantic delusions,
that you're just fleshy
versions of your own Stiquito,
the android mosquito,
you invented by yourselves
to fetch ping pong balls
all day in a laboratory,
triggered by radio waves
it obeys but cannot feel.
Here in my void, far above
the universe I made
by rubbing together some stars
off my enormous robe
until they exploded in a bang,
I'm frowning and pacing,
deciding what I should do.
Shall I wipe you all out
or just leave you alone?
It's hard to think up here,
surrounded by noisy angels
standing inside one another,
debating the size of nothing.

A SECRET LIFE

A Thought went up my mind today—
That I have had before—
        —Emily Dickinson

I'm one of your oldest Thoughts, playful, bright,
shaped like an expanding, rainbowed bubble
blown through a wand—until I shrink and vanish.
I rent a small house inside your brain
built on the great fault between the known and unknown
where the plates slide and rub, and I'm waiting
for you to think of me again
so I can rise in all my shimmering colors.
But you don't. I'm banished to the cellar,
one of the angelic ones shoved down here
with the unspeakable in their masks and fur capes
who growl at times, and press their shoulders
against the locked door, trying to scare you.

I remember those airy flights when you first
thought me, how I shone and trembled, attracting
amazement and praise. How happy we were together.
Now I attend the funerals of your lost Memories,
and hold hands with the rest, shrunken and sad,
repeating their little bit of story,
trying to be the ones to live in you forever.
I don't tell them that they're only holograms
constructed from us Thoughts. I tell myself
I'm essential, hardly distinguishable from your body,
but I'm worried at the silence, all the cells
shutting down in your brain, and the young Thoughts
breaking into your flickering Dream Theater
to hook an image you'll recall at dawn,
attracted to the flashy, sexy ones in boots.

Once, cleaning out your drawers, you found
your tangled baby locket, and I could feel
stirrings in your heart as you tried to unknot
the thin, gold chain you'd worn with your pinafore

at the age of one, denting the heart with your teeth
while you cooed at your piece of birthday cake.
I stood on tiptoe, believing you'd think me
back into your mind, your brilliant early Thought,
the one that lit your face with a smile
captured by a snapshot, so tender and pure
your parents made copies for every relative.
But you frowned, and I felt myself sinking back
into oblivion. I hardly know what I am,
the house above me loud with heavy steps
as the new tenants take possession in your brain,
pulling my simple pictures off the walls,
throwing my fairy tales into the garbage bin.

COMPUTER MAP OF THE EARLY UNIVERSE

We're made of stars. The scientific team
Flashes a blue and green computer chart
Of the universe across my T. V. screen
To prove its theory with a work of art:
Temperature shifts translated into waves
Of color, numbers hidden in smooth lines.
 "At last we have a map of ancient Time"
One scientist says, lost in a rapt gaze.
I look at the bright model they've designed,
The Big Bang's fury frozen into laws,
Pleased to see it resembles a sonnet,
A little frame of images and rhyme
That tries to glitter brighter than its flaws
And trick the truth into its starry net.

THREE RED PEARS

Slicing across the pear with the largest bruise,
    I imagine an Oregon orchard by the sea
Where these three hung, bright with roseate dew,
    Before the packing crate and rumbling boxcar
Brought them to my hometown grocery store.
    I liked their speckled skin and tapered shape
So I bought them, though they felt unyielding
    When I squeezed them. Now when I eat a chunk
I'm surprised at the sweet taste of the flesh
    For I thought they'd rotted past ripening
While I was busy with my books and papers,
    Trying to finish dull mounds of work
I hated, reports, dissections of people
    Spread out on committee tables like frogs,
My forehead furrowed, and my pulse too fast.

But today the pears are perfect in my mouth.
    As I swallow the last piece and wash the knife
I hope that underneath my human skin
    Chemicals are turning bile to sugar,
That after weeks of saying "Yes" to "No,"
    Trying to Right the implacable armored Wrong
That rules and swaggers, I won't have rotted,
    My heart veined and pitted with disease
Like the hearts of the old men, my colleagues,
    Bathed in the ichor of forty long years
Of struggle over an anthill for ant spoils,
    Who now enter hospitals for by-pass surgery
Or collapse red-faced in the elevator.
    Please heart, slow down, remember long ago
You were a baby's heart, you were my own,
    And long before you were anybody's heart
There was just an orchard under the sun,
    Pear trees in bloom, radiance from the boughs
Blinding, transparent, like an angel's wing.

FAUX DEER

Once, hiking a ridge line in October woods,
I held my breath, surprised to spot a doe
turning to gaze at me. She didn't leap
across my path, and disappear in the brush,
so I dared a step, and then another step,
wishing I could stroke her velvet nose,
or murmur endearments into her big ears.
That's when I found she was a rigged-up decoy,
set up to fool the poachers. She'd been shot
over and over, her hide seared with bullets.
I shivered to think of someone sighting along
a rifle barrel from the ravine below,
and ran back to the trail, forgetting her
on the drive home. But today I remember
my spoiled hike as I read this news story,
DEER DECOYS CATCH POACHERS IN ACT.
Our state now has sixteen look-alikes
with detachable antlers that can revise
a buck into a doe, and other creatures,
fake owls, eagles, coyotes, hawks, wild turkeys
posing as game, hidden in the state parks.
In the AP photo, conservation officers
carry Artie out of the bare grey woods
for repair. He's in pieces, his antlered head
unswiveled from his lacerated trunk.
I stare at the scene, trying to match it
to some lost feeling, that dreamy moment
before I grasped the danger we were in
and simply stood there in childlike wonder
at the magic deer, unafraid of me,
who seemed to have stepped from a fairy tale
where animals talk, and humans understand.

PIG

Washing dishes, my mother at the store,
Her kitchen unchanged since I used to place
My ring with the glass ruby heart on a ledge
And plunge my hands into the soapy water,
I watched a blank fog drift over the snow.
I listened to the sounds of the empty house
Until it seemed I'd never lived my life,
Was still a child, dreaming of this future.
Yet each visit home I found things missing,
Old dolls, textbooks, yellowed straw hats. . .
I let the water drain, squeezed out the sponge,
Then climbed to the attic. My figure skates
No longer hung by their laces on a peg,
So more of me was gone—not that I wanted
To take the stuff with me. I wanted it here,
For when I rescued or saved anything,
And took it back to my own far away house,
It turned to dusty junk. Beside a pile
Of games I found my old ceramic bank,
A little pig with cheerful eyelashes
Named Pansy. Inside her curved body,
Painted with flowers, I'd saved my allowance
In dimes and pennies for Christmas presents.
The hole where you shook coins out again
Was nicked and worn, and I remembered
Using a hairpin to work the last ones out.
Standing there, my hands around the smooth pig,
I shivered and wondered what to do with her
For part of me was hiding inside her
Like a genie in a lamp, waiting patiently
For someone to make the third and final wish.
I looked down into the chipped slot. It seemed
As if the pig breathed at my touch, and yet
She'd turn to nothing if I took her away
To stand on my mantel, another knickknack.
Yet how easily she could vanish in this attic
As year by year my mother swept me out.

I thought and wondered, hating the sentimental
But gripped by waves of it like stomach flu.
I hid her behind the scratched Glenn Miller records
Stored after my father's death, covered by
My sister's drawings from her first art class.
Back downstairs, I had to splash cold water
Over my burning face to hide my emotion,
Pathetic and childish, but strong as a weed.

THE ORIGIN OF FLOWERING PLANTS

Some say the first flower, complex, waxy,
bloomed from the shrubby magnolia.
Others believe that certain herbs
put forth simple blossoms along river banks
so tiny the browsing dinosaurs
missed them as they chewed.
I vote for the herbs. Magnolias are baroque,
complicated and showy. When I lived in the South,
I'd walk down avenues of huge magnolia trees
crunching the fallen leaves, where they were strewn
like curled banana peels under the branches.
I'd admire the large saucers of the blossoms,
astonished by beauty displayed on a scale
that seemed to exclude me with its perfection.
Here in the North, where I live now,
the ground greens slowly with tender shoots
so transparent you can only see them
when you get down on your hands and knees to look,
scraping back dead grass to find, here and there,
a delicate stigma inside a cup of petals.
Imagine being the ancestral angiosperm—
that rumbling thunder shaking your riverbank
must be the slap of the dinosaur's tail
as it whacks the trees and shrubs in its path.
Your diminutive flower quivers on its stalk,
the carpel bulging with the earth's first
mysterious new seeds. You've made them
by yourself, but how? What are they for?
Soon the shadow of a neck blots out the sun,
and teeth rake over the tough, wet stalks
swaying above you, and you feel your whole self,
all your struggling growth, your mastery,
pressed down into a layer of the clay
where centuries will turn you into fossil.
Now the massive hind legs gouge a pit,
the river seeps in, but the shock
freed your seeds—sealed, half-aquatic, they float.

Later, when the water dries up in the sun
leaving silky mud down in the pit,
a few seeds flourish, remembering you
in every gene as they burst into existence,
unnoticed, shy, but radiant with the future.

SEARCHES

Once again TV detectives are searching the suspects' rooms in
some old rambling house in England. The Chief Inspector opens
the bureau drawers in tiers, pulling out striped ties and folded
white shirts; he sniffs every cut-glass bottle; he ruffles
through papers on the desk, unclasps a small leather book and
turns unerringly to the suspicious entry. In another room his
tweed-coated assistant pushes back filmy dresses, and holds up a
black high heel checking for traces of a red garden clay. "Why
is there a dead wasp on the nightstand," he wonders aloud, while
his superior calls him across the hall. "Why has someone thrown
a glass of brandy into the fireplace?" Red herrings, these
questions will never be answered, but the two men exchange
knowing looks as the musical score, something in imitation of
Elgar, swells in excitement. Downstairs in a library of
mullioned windows and walls of gilt-stamped books, the impatient
suspects drink sherry and smoke cigarettes, their faces
twitching, their eyes shifty or worried or insouciant. Later,
alone here in my own room, I wonder if I have any secrets from
myself, and I open my top drawer briskly to see who this person
is who calls herself by my name. What's this? All these
curious hair ornaments, barrettes, tortoise shell combs, silvery
elastic bands. Here's a snood; here are chiffon ribbons and
satin ribbons; a box full of black bobby pins with blunt plastic
tips and another containing thin sharp spidery hairpins; here's
an ancient torn hairnet for blonds; here's an unopened package
containing a nylon flexible comb tossed on top of jeweled pony-
tail holders, a lime-plastic device for creating a French roll,
a spongy nylon doughnut for a bun, and more barrettes, some
cloisonne, others burnished metal. Oh how unerringly a
detective's hands sort through this distracting clutter! The
camera zooms in on a small box of "Bronchial-Pastillen" from the
Hertenstein Drogerie in Luzern, Switzerland. Throat lozenges or
cyanide tablets? I'm as surprised as the audience when I pry
open the tin lid to discover a catch of fifty yellowed slips
saved from the centers of crisp fortune cookies devoured years
ago in forgotten Chinese restaurants. What can it mean? The
camera moves in on my expression. Another red herring? Or the real
clue to her existence?

II / MOUNTAIN SUITE

BELLA TOLA

I

"If I could only turn my self to vapor
And drift above that steep hillside of pine
Or cross that range of glacial mountain peaks
Changing my shape, now billowy, now wispy,
I'm sure," she said, "you'd never hear me sigh."
Who was listening? That bird, that purple flower?
She was alone on the balcony watching clouds.
Time to speak to the bees sucking cow parsley,
To the browsing horses,to the pure Alpine air.
She'd twisted her foot climbing Bella Tola,
And now sat immobile, her ankle swollen,
Far above the world. "Trapped here in heaven
Like a saint who's just arrived, still woozy,
Who hasn't gotten the knack of cloud-walking
And keeps sinking through to his knobby knees
So that patrolling angels have to swoop
Over him, pulling him up by the armpits."

She felt as if she'd been pulled up by the armpits.

"Poor saint. He's got to forget it all,
Those years of hair-shirts and flagellations,
The lonely cave, where lepers sought him out
Asking him to bless their shriveling flesh,
And especially those lithe dancing girls
Sent by the devil on hot summer nights
Brushing their nipples across his mouth, whipping
His scabbed back with their braided hair.
That's over with. Another step, and yet another,
Then whoosh, he's tumbled through again
Up to his mouth in gauzy cloud, which clings
To his beard as the angels drag him up
For another lecture on forgetfulness."

Why, she must have dozed off! Bright clouds
Have vanished, and the mountain's pumping fog
As if there's a big machine on the other side,
The kind they have in musicals so dancers
Can swirl across an illusory heaven.
"Illusory? Real enough for Fred and Ginger
To step down from the choir, and sneak out
The back gate to dance across those peaks
Maybe forgetting their names, but not missing
A step together as they sway and turn,
Memory locked inside their ghostly ankles."

She's spoken, but no one hears her. She hums.
Her waltz is so off key it makes her smile.

"Memory locked inside." She repeats her phrase,
Scaring the bird who's been watching from the rafters
Of the chalet. It flies up. In a flash—
Is it her words, or the bird's fluttery dart—
She's remembered what made her sad last week,
Colossal statues outside Prague Castle,
Enormous stone men, muscular, ruthless,
One clubbing a foe to death, his granite arm
Frozen for centuries in its murderous swing,
The other piercing a shoulder with his sword,
And beneath them, ephemeral citizens
Passing back and forth on the worn cobblestones
Shadowed by the raised, reflexive arms,
The sinewy, twisted backs, the brute stares
That lock terror deep in human memory.

III

But the higher you climb, she thinks, the less
You remember. At the top of Bella Tola,
Out of breath, sweating, palms scratched by rocks,
During her five minutes of vertigo, or panic,
When the trail disappeared into a snowbank,
And she'd had to find a route across the scree
Moving in a crouch, her chest heaving,
Forcing herself to go an inch, then another,
Not looking down at the dizzying drop off
Into hazy vastness, but reaching up and up
Until she pulled herself over the ledge
Of the summit, where a metal cross was cemented,
(And many others, who'd climbed the easier side,
Sprawled on rocks eating chocolate bars, viewing
The fabled glacier, a sea of glistening ice)
She had felt like a giant on the earth
Spread below her into separate valleys,
The Val d'Anniviers, and the Turtmanntal,
One speaking French and the other German.
She had no past, no future, not even a body
Gulping thin air, shivering as it cooled.
"I was ego, bobbing this way and that
Like a Mylar balloon painted with my face
Thrilled by its own valiant existence
Full of a gas lighter than air, taller
Than the puny person holding it up
By a silver ribbon. I dreamed more,
Saw more, felt more than the others
Snapping each other's pictures on the summit
Or eating apples, rubbing their aching knees
As they consulted maps. Only *I* was free
To float, pure thought, into the ether."

She said this to the bird, who'd flown back
Attracted to her lack of motion. She laughed.
That was before she'd fallen going down
Turning her ankle so sharply she understood
She was herself, her past returned to her

BEN NEVIS

"Read me a lesson, Muse, and speak it loud
Upon the top of Nevis, blind in mist!"

Did Keats sit here or there
to write his sonnet? The chasm
drops away. Below the air
shimmers with auto exhaust

and hikers strip off shirts,
pinking their backs in the sun.
I've climbed a shadeless trail
sweating and gasping

with hundreds of other people
coming up from the car park,
fathers in bill caps, mothers
tugging children by the hand,

old men, red-faced and wobbly
leaning on ski poles, everyone
sharing inadequate water
surprised by such violent heat

so that some cupped their hands
in falling stream trickles
below sheep folds. I thought
I was climbing up out of Hell

until I reached the top.
The hotel had not been built
when Keats slogged up here;
now it's already a ruin,

a pile of tumbled down rocks
filled with lager cans,
biscuit wrappers, toilet paper—
the world's ugliest summit,

rocks and debris, sewer pipe,
dirty patches of snow,
and, from a pitched orange tent,
amplified drums, screamed lyrics.

August 2, 1818—yearning
for the Beautiful, sad Keats
chaffed his cold hands,
blinded by the Scottish mist,

and remembered Burns's cottage:
"O the flummery of a birth place!
Cant! Cant! Cant!"
This is what he'd longed for,

his own peak in Darien,
grandeur and shortness of breath
mixed up until he felt dizzy
like a long night reading Homer.

He stepped nearer the edge
where the cliff disappeared
into a cloud, or was it steam
rising up from a lake in Hell?

Alarmed, Brown called him back
and he turned, shuddering,
not yet daring to hear
an answer from the sullen mist.

So he sat down, his throat sore,
took off his stiff boots,
and dutifully smoothed paper
over his knee. And wrote.

HAPPINESS

Today you're going to hike to the very end
Of this steep valley, where the path rises
And disappears beyond the waterfall
Marked on the yellow sign you saw last night
Before you went to sleep to dream of today.
Now, as you yawn here on the balcony
Of the chalet, you hear distant cowbells.
Clouds drift off to reveal the mighty glacier
Glittering in the folds of limestone peaks.
The fields around you are already half in sun,
Spangled with cow parsley and blue flowers,
So pinch yourself. This isn't a dream at all.
Go on, take that crooked path by the monastery,
And cross the meadow where the brothers' cows
Browse near the haystacks. Let the morning dew
Brush against your legs, and don't be afraid
Of distracted bees who come to smell your pollen.
Your path winds up among the wild flowers,
Brilliant carpets of purple and yellow stars
Cut by the flash of swiftly running streams.
Don't forget to open and shut each gate,
And greet the cows cropping the high pastures
Below the moraine. You can rest on a boulder
As big as a house, swept down years ago
From waves of ice bright on the ridge above,
But you must keep walking to the valley's end,
Ignoring the signs for trails that lead to summits
Crowded with tourists riding the cable car,
Beer gardens, grottos, or sculptured ice caves.
You're heading for that wall of wind-swept granite
Already casting a shadow over the fields
Where bony cows graze on the last, thin grass,
And when you arrive, you'll shiver with pleasure,
Delighted by the small, white-washed chapel,
And the farmhouse close to the famous pass
Where a herder's family eats at a trestle table
Under an apple tree. But you must be careful

40

As you approach. This is the one moment
When happiness could be blown from your grasp
Like a child's balloon, so you must guard it,
Not release it with a sigh or a groan
By looking up above the waterfall,
And wishing you could cross the dangerous pass.
You have no grappling hooks. It's getting cold.
That's fog blowing in sheets over the ridge,
Thunder booming from the vanished gorge.
Now you must bravely turn your back forever
On the outskirts of what's impossible,
And return without regret to your calm life,
Content to remember your long, perfect day.
For if you start to climb that perilous trail
As I see you doing now, your smile gone,
Your heart pounding as you brace your shoulders,
Determined to find a way up through the mist
Who will follow you, who will lead you back?

CROAGH PATRICK

"This holy ground
No place for litter"

I watched him pour his tea
into his saucer to cool
as he talked about the curse
on our family for drowning a landlord

in the lough behind Toureen,
and the Big Storm of 1881
that had drowned his own grandparents
on the Ballinrobe road.

He kept his gun and holster
next to the Infant of Prague
on the dresser. Once he pinned
his silver badge on my collar

and I danced around the kitchen
while he sang about Finnegan
sitting up in his coffin,
and praised the rose of Tralee.

He said he'd climbed Croagh Patrick
barefoot, his feet bleeding
to get a plenary indulgence
and cancel years in Purgatory

before he sailed for America.
He'd named my father Patrick—
my father, nostalgic for Ireland
all his life in the Midwest,

too busy raising nine children
to come here until he was sick,
his heart too weak to climb
this hill. So I'm doing it

for him. Panting, I turn
but Clew Bay's vanished in mist.
Below me a few hikers
toil up the steep scree

in slickers, nylon hoods,
but no one's barefoot, or kneeling
humbly on the windy summit,
pelted by gusts of sleet,

and my own hands, cold claws,
do not fold in prayer
though father and grandfather
clutched rosaries in their coffins;

but as I dig in my pocket
for my last piece of chocolate,
a tissue goes flying off.
A believer in holy ground,

I scramble after it,
startling mountain sheep
who run on thin black legs
down the same pilgrim track

my grandfather hobbled up
that far off day, his sins
absolved, his offspring
charged inside him like ions

inside a sudden, violent cloud.
Here's thunder, here's lightning,
here's me on the mountain
like a strike from his brain.

ICEMAN

The T.V. camera pans across a body
hikers found beneath a melting glacier.
Five thousand years ago this lake dweller
climbed the mountain above his village
just like I do every summer, and his goal
wasn't commerce, some trade in flint,
as the commentator insists, it was
simply a beautiful day when he set out
and the mysterious peaks drew him up.
Caught in a snowstorm, he burrowed down
into a crevice where he died from cold.
Now two countries claim his remains.
Though his penis and scrotum are missing
after picks freed him from the ice,
he's a prize of Neolithic chemicals.
I like his leather pouch of sloeberries
for they look like the blueberries bagged
inside my own freezer, and his unstrung bow
suggests he wasn't going too far, he meant
to turn back at every step, but the view
ravished him, and he followed the goat path
higher and higher with untipped arrows
and a useless bow, until the clouds moved
swiftly across the glittering blue limestone,
and he shivered, looked back. Now we see
he had charcoal tattoos striping his back
and knees, grass stuffed into his shoes
of sewn leather, and two dried mushrooms
hanging from a string. Is this the afterlife?
One man survives his tribe and family
keeping his human shape, even his skin,
though his eye jelly's gone, and his dreams
have evaporated from the frozen brain
sliced under the microscope. The star
that once exploded to make him, still shines,
for his body protein emits radiation,
just a little, but enough to date him.

When I turn off the set, I hear the wind
clicking sleet against the windowpanes.
In six months I'll walk the Iceman's trails
into the Alps, where the heart melts,
and if I only believed in five thousand years
to come, I would prepare to arrive there.
I'd choose an object, and I'd drop it
into the crevice of a deep, rippled glacier—
something scribbled down in my own writing.
or a ring with my name inside for easy fame.

III/SHAKESPEARE AND COMPANY

OUTSIDE ST.-REMY-DE-PROVENCE

Where are the grand olives with gnarled bark
That Van Gogh painted a hundred years ago?
These little trees rustle as if in talk,
Newly planted along the ancient rows.
Beyond, I see the clinique of St. Paul
Where Van Gogh wrestled madness into art
And broke this landscape into molecules
That make us dizzy. He took it all apart.

Today it's only pretty, tame and small.
In the garden I look for his portrait bust
Sculpted after his death, but nothing's there.
A sign says vandals have destroyed it. Appalled
I gaze at the pedestal covered with dust—
And nothing stares at me with his mad stare.

SIMULTANEOUS

Halloween. Passengers on the propjet commuter plane circling
Chicago turn over pages in fat novels with embossed covers, or
murmur to one another about missed connections, or close their
eyes, thinking of home, the one they've left behind or the one
they're so close to, just down there below the turbulent clouds
that make their stomachs churn. The molded plastic purple skull
ring, worn for a joke, flashes on my finger as I gesture in the
classroom which seems to grow brighter as the sky darkens
outside, and thunder rumbles. In her office, a colleague looks
up from reading, thinking of her husband flying through such
weather. An angel with foil-covered wings, and a vampire in a
black rayon cape, each carrying a paper shopping bag, hurry up
the walk to my front door, but since I'm not home, no one
answers. A bolt of lightning makes the students at the seminar
table look up, laugh nervously, and pass around the paper plate
of candy corn and tiny marzipan pumpkins somebody has brought to
class, held during the town's official hours for trick or
treating. "Hurry up, you guys," a father calls out, while the
angel bangs harder at my door. "It's going to pour any
minute." A man driving on Route 55 spots a black puff of smoke,
and sees a plane banking sharply before it plunges to the
ground. The wind rattles windows and bends trees just as
someone praises the beauty of a certain line of poetry. The
angel crouches inside her father's car as the rain streams down
the windshield, her wings mashed against the car seat, while the
vampire takes off his mask, wet from his own breath, and wipes
the lipstick blood off his mouth. Thunder booms, and the sky
cracks with brilliant light. One of my cats claws under the
mattress liner, and burrows into the box springs, while the
other crouches in the dark living room, watching the front door,
her tail quivering. In a soybean field sixty eight hearts and
one hundred and eighty two pieces of luggage explode at the same
moment. My colleague looks at her watch, hoping her husband
will call soon. Up and down my street, rain extinguishes the
candles burning in the grinning jack-o'-lanterns set out on
front steps. Fourteen students and one teacher look again at a
line of poetry, some of us agreeing that it is beautiful, some

of us doubting it, and some of us just looking nervously over our shoulders at our reflections on the shaking glass.

BLUE RUNNING SHOES

At first I thought someone had trashed a grave
when I glimpsed a pair of worn running shoes
tossed in the grass, laces knotted together.

I stopped to read the thick, polished headstone,
and saw the brass medallion of an athlete
stamped into the granite, the word "brother"

carved below the name of a young man
dead at nineteen. These were his shoes,
worn Nikes, nylon stitched to blue suede,

and I imagined a younger brother
sneaking out here at night to leave them
so they wouldn't be packed up for GoodWill.

Had he been killed on that roaring Interstate
that ran beside this rambling cemetery,
right next to the motel I'd just checked into?

I jogged on in the dusk, and soon got lost
down some winding, hemlock shadowed path.
That's when I first began to hear somebody

coming up fast behind me, breathing hard.
Looking over my shoulder, I saw a runner
burst from the gauzy twilight into focus,

his mouth wide open as he gasped for air,
face pearled with effort, hair slicked back.
He came abreast of me, almost flying,

every detail of him sharp and clear
for just one moment before the cooling mist
blurred him to indistinctness as he ran

beyond me, out of my sight. I'd like to say
I recognized his running shoes at once,
could swear to you they were the same pair

I'd seen on the grave, but he was gone
past me too quickly. I don't believe in ghosts
but someone did, or half-did, anyway.

I stiffened when I heard that runner's steps
coming fast behind me. Afraid, or what?
I couldn't say, and yet, my heart revived

when I saw that sweat-bathed living face,
just some young fellow flashing past me,
urging his burning body through the gloom.

GIFTS

Lilac, lavender, lily of the valley—
I lift the soap up to my face.
I'm Christmas shopping for my aunt,
who's forced to discontinue chemo,
hardly able to keep food down.
I used to send her panettone,
boxes of glazed apricots,
or lavish travel books on Ireland—
things I thought a nun would like
to unwrap after Midnight mass.
But the many worldly objects
I've fingered in a dozen shops—
hand blown glass, engagement books,
tote bags stenciled with sleeping cats—
seemed so wrong I stepped into
this fragrance store for inspiration.
And yet a wave of guilt chokes me
as I give my credit card to a clerk
for this little stack of boxes,
wildflowers sealed in glycerin,
hand-milled distilled carnations,
lanolin ovals of English violet.
Is this to be my final gift?
The clerk hands the card back.
My thumb runs over the numbers
embossed on the slick front,
and with a tingle I remember
stroking my aunt's holy cards
enclosed with childhood birthday presents,
pictures of Mary dressed in blue
bending over the swaddled child,
or martyrs smiling serenely
from the rack, their legs broken.
My favorite scene was Jesus
surprising his mother in the Temple,
his expression rapt and tender
as he taught the amazed elders.

I'd stroke the textured halos
around the sacred heads, as if
sanctity might rub off on me
absorbed through my human skin.
Now it's only money's ghost
I touch, slipping my card
back with others into my wallet,
before I grab the paper bag
off the glass counter, hoping
in spite of my devouring gloom
that my aunt's face is shining
like the saints, that this soap
smells to her of heavenly gardens.

for Sr. Coletta M. Stanton, BVM, 1922-1994

AGAINST THE GRAVE

Cynthia, last night I saw you
standing outside your office,
and I started walking towards you,
surprised by your reproachful face.
Your lips moved. I couldn't hear you,
but I followed your troubled gesture,
looking past you, or through you,
not understanding myself
why the office was cold and bare,
the desktop smooth with dust,
and the chair turned upside down.

I'm awake now, glad my dream
conjured you back so vividly.
Caught in the web of my brain
you tow thousands behind you,
all the loved ones you remember,
your aunts and your father,
then all the ones they remember, too,
dear parents, brothers and sisters
lost in the nineteenth century,
a palimpsest of human faces
some scholar of the supernatural
might trace back for generations
like the evolution of bird song.
After they bolt my own casket,
you'll exist inside me, too,
and if anyone dreams me back,
I'll haunt them as long as I can,
trying to drag you up
with your cats, Maxwell and Charlie,
my hand in your ghostly hand.

for Cynthia Jordan, 1948-1993

THE DRESSING ROOM

Communion dresses hung on a special rack
Near "Women's Coats" and "Ladies' Lingerie."
My mother chose three that floated like clouds,
And in the dressing room I tried them on.
I loved the flounces, sashes, puffy sleeves,
But didn't notice the unraveled hems,
Or missing pearl buttons. My mother sighed.
She told me to wait, and went to look for others,
So I twirled before the mirror in my slip
Thinking of everything I'd wear next Sunday,
White veil, white patent leather shoes, white socks.
I combed and fluffed my bangs with my fingers,
Then heard a funny moan that made me jump.
I put my eye to the seam between the curtains
Dividing the dressing room into cubicles.
An old woman was taking off her clothes,
The skin flapping from her upper arms
As she tugged her dress up to her wrinkled neck
And over her grey bun. Her speckled hands
Shook, pulling at the cloth to free her head,
Revealing a hunched back spotted with moles.
Her legs, where her girdle had ridden up,
Were blue with swollen veins, almost as if
Snakes were crawling upward to her heart.
I'd never seen an old woman's body
And I wondered if I'd look like that someday,
Crooked and bent, my flesh melting away.
Then, in the mirror, our eyes met. She flushed
And grabbed a polka-dot blouse from a chair,
Holding it against her sagging breasts
As she turned to confront me. I ducked away,
Terrified she'd yell, or call my mother,
And in that second her shame and outrage
Scorched my memory. Yet she did nothing.
I only heard her rustling behind the curtain
As I stood with my back to my own mirror,
Afraid to look at my vanishing image.

When my mother returned with another dress,
I trembled at the touch of her calloused fingers
Tying the ribbon around my tender neck.

THE WALL

Knocking lightly against my study door,
The tile men ask me to come and verify
Damage to the wall beside my bathtub.
They've ripped away the moldy tile and found
Not only rotting wood, but an ants' nest,
Constructed from the soft, chewable boards.
I don't want to see this, but I must,
And follow their white uniforms upstairs.
The wall gapes like a wound, dark, smelly,
Swarming with frantic ants. I swallow hard,
Listening to the boss speak of solutions,
New two-by-fours, exterminators, wall board.
I look at the inner structure of my house,
Remembering how I showered just that morning,
Shampooing my hair, my elbow brushing the tile
Only an inch from this pulsing, shadowy world.

Hard to return to my desk. How meaningless
All my intricate, scribbled words appear
Balanced against the ants' doomed colony
And my instinctive need to save my house
Which makes me stay shut up here, but aware
Of every curious noise on the floor above.
The exterminator comes and sprays and goes,
I hear the slam of hammers, the low swish
Of compounds mixed with water from the tap,
And the workmen's radio where every song
Recounts the loneliness of long-haul truckers.
I stare down at a page of looping doodles
Trying not to think of my brisk orders
To kill the ants who burrowed in my wood,
But all my black-ink letters look like legs
On stricken bodies soon to be walled in
With tile so bright I may even see myself
Reflected darkly as I grab for the soap.

VISIBLE MAN

I spot him next to a hobnail glass bowl
at the Antique Mall. He sports a price tag
like china urns and silver sugar tongs.
Stepping closer, I see he's lost his heart,
though all his other organs seem intact
under the clear shell of yellowed plastic
only a foot high. I stroke his bald head
where the grooved brain fits like a walnut,
thinking how I'm more like him every year.
I'm one of those who let passers-by see
through to the inner mess. And yet for years
I admired his opposite, the Invisible Man,
the one whose body can't be seen at all
as he steps through French windows from the terrace
(the curtains billow), and joins the bad guys
at the cocktail party. A martini glass
floats up from the butler's silver tray,
tips back, and gin flows into the air,
disappearing. I thought by now I'd be
invisible, too, able to move unseen
in crowds, but even if I drink an elixir
promising transparency, it wears off
in public at the wrong time, revealing
a trembling throat, a disembodied hand.
So here's the one I really resemble,
this small, stiff man I used to take apart
on the kitchen table, separating bones
and muscles from the liver and the lungs
before I grew impatient, my fingers clumsy,
and worked to stuff the parts inside again
upside down, backwards, or any old way
to give the illusion he was still whole
under the peepshow of his plastic skin.

OUT-PATIENT SURGERY

Remember science fiction comic strips
that claimed we'd be all be immaterial
by the year 2000? I liked the panels
where the artist drew somebody shut in a booth
jabbing at buttons to send a vaporous
dream-self into the arms of an illusion
created by somebody else hidden from sight.
Why, nothing could hurt a shape that drifted
like a cloud, no knife could slice into
what wasn't there.
                        Waiting for surgery,
I think each of us would like to stay behind
while a simulacrum climbed onto the stretcher
for the ride down to the operating room.
In hospital gowns and funny slipper socks,
we sit among relatives in street clothes
looking pale and strange, like holograms
projected out of our tossing nightmares.
"I didn't sleep last night," a bald man says.
". . . slept poorly," a woman sighs behind me.
Once it was six a.m. Now it's later,
but my watch is locked away.
                              A television
flashes the local news in the corner
and everyone shifts to hear about the accident
caused by ice on the same roads we traveled
to get here. But the man who survived
his car skidding into the Interstate ditch
was hit by another car as he flagged down help,
run over by a third, and then a fourth,
making us all shudder, and draw deep breaths
of pity, mixed with relief that we're alive
in spite of all our dread of being here.
Beside me, a woman groans. Her husband
clasps her hand. A tall man dressed like me
rises at the sound of his name. He looks back
almost longingly at his empty chair,

61

then squares his shoulders and pads from the room,
prepared to follow his body where it goes,
his dream-self locked inside its cage of bone.

AH, CLEO

Cleo came back from the dead in my dream.
I was surprised to see her, and I gasped,
"Cleo, my God! You're looking sleek and fat."

"Not skinny like before I croaked, you mean?"
She smiled the way cats do, her eyes lit
Spectrally from behind with a yellow glow.

"Well, yes," I said, surprised she could talk.
I longed to pick her up for a nice hug,
But what if my hands cut through her like smoke?

"They would," she grinned, reading my thoughts
As she arched her back. "I'm only a shade.
In fact the underworld is filled with cats.

We glide and shimmy in the darkness with
No difficulty, while you humans blunder
And stumble, complaining in loud voices

That echo up and down Hell's long hallways,
Disturbing us. We cats are sensitive to noise.
All our lives we listen to you whine

Purring hard to soothe your constant dismay
At everything that happens, rainy days,
Letters that didn't come, the boss's shit,

Head colds, PMS, and the serious stuff,
Depression, quarrels, death. I'll admit
Your lives are long enough to be sad.

So are ours, they just seem to go faster.
Afterwards, what's the difference? We're the same.
But there are more of us, fewer of you.

So please, a little consideration, please.
Keep it down. A howl or two, OK,
But not that constant, ancient yammering

Of bitter reproach, those useless curses.
A trillion mice act with more dignity."
Then Cleo raised a paw, and licked it once,

Saluting me. "You always were my favorite.
See you around, but not soon, I hope."
She winked and vanished. "Ah, Cleo!" I sighed.

WINTER WALK

One winter night, faces hidden in scarves,
We two tramped out across the snowy park
Down in the dumps about most everything,
When all at once we glimpsed a snow angel
Brushed into the hillside we were climbing,
A small, shallow shape just visible
In the moonlight. We stopped, and you exclaimed
You'd never actually seen one before,
Though I'd stretched out across a snowdrift once
To show you the technique. But I was heavy,
And jumping to my feet, left the outline
Of someone knocked down, murdered, dragged away.
But here was a perfect child-sized angel
(Boy or girl, no way on earth to tell)
Like a rare intaglio in the deep snow,
And we cheered up, thinking it an omen.
Next night, the weather still cold, we followed
The same path, and there it was, untrampled,
Though now surrounded by many boot prints
Of others who had stepped carefully around
On smooth or waffled soles. I thought about
All the people who'd paused here just like us
Looking down at the angel, so personal
(the child's cap had a tassel at its tip)
And yet, somehow, so strangely anonymous—
If we could only make a mark like that
When we die, whirling our arms into wings.

SHAKESPEARE AND COMPANY

In this curled snapshot, I stand outside Shakespeare and
Company between two American poets. All three of us are
smiling at a Hollywood director, the wife of one of the poets,
who is snapping the picture. But she's not visible. Even if
you trace our eyebeams to a point beyond the frame, and try to
reconstruct her as a three-dimensional hologram existing just
at the spot where a miniature sized viewer of this photograph
might stand, shrunken to thumb size, you won't be able to
visualize her. But this is what she saw that Sunday in Paris.
On the sidewalk, a red motor bike with a wooden crate strapped
on behind blocks any view of the lower legs of the poets.
Behind them, through the wavy glass of the tall, dark framed
windows, a chandelier lights up the walls of books in the
interior where some shadowy figures are browsing. A few
minutes before, the three poets looked for their own books
inside the shop, but did not find them. So now they are
standing beneath the letters of the signboard SHAKESPEARE AND
COMPANY. A large engraving of Shakespeare's face looks down at
them in the space between the E of SHAKESPEARE and the A of
AND. These poets, wishing to be identified as of the company,
have clustered themselves under the longer word, SHAKESPEARE,
aware that the address of this bookshop has changed since
the days of Joyce and Pound and Sylvia Beach. The poets know that
only the big, nostalgic letters over their heads are important
in this composition that is in the process of being hurtled
into the future with a snap of the shutter, along with their
insouciance in standing here, grinning with irony, but
determined to exist in this juxtaposition for as long as the
chemicals are bound to this brief paper.

CYBER-LOVE

In The Tale of Genji everyone writes poems
by quoting famous poems, adding new lines
about the moon, or heartvine, or sea grass.

If you're sorrowing, speak of your wet sleeves.
If you're lonely, describe brine on driftwood.
When your wife dies, you can't bear to look upon

her pillow, the sheets she slept beneath;
and so you choose some dark mist-grey paper,
your best brush, and step into the garden

to let the thousand poems you know by heart
well up inside you. At last some classic line
about a cedar tree, or a crane in the clouds

tears you apart, and you begin to imagine
her face again as you sit down to write,
blending your own sad voice with the poet's.

Or maybe you write to your lover. She sends
a reply, attached to a chrysanthemum bud,
and when you unfold her pale lavender paper

you find a little poem echoing another,
in distinguished calligraphy, the old words
radiant with the new like a fresh iris.

And sometimes you never meet the hidden one
whose delicate heart resembles your own,
but you keep writing, almost as if to yourself,

describing exile on the windswept seashore,
the dew-chilled rushes, the salt burners
down on the strand in their reed-roofed huts.

Your unknown beloved, so distant, unfolds
your words, lets them sink into his depths
where other words well up from the turmoil

as he writes of wild geese, or ruined bridges
where branches twine above a muddy river—
and here I am, centuries later, reading

their words as if they were buried bulbs
or light still traveling from a long dead star.
It reminds me of passing the computer cluster

on campus yesterday when I put the book down.
While sparrows ate buds off the pear trees
with quick, scissoring beaks, and spring grass

brightened beneath long runners of forsythia,
I saw shadowy figures hunched in the room
before screens, faces dreamy and engrossed.

Were they romancing each other on e-mail,
or searching Finders for someone to love on-line?
I imagined fingers flicking across keyboards

as rapturous words scrolled past, strangers
speaking to strangers of their dreams
unencumbered by the ancient, dangerous body.

Delete, Cancel, or press Send? A burning
lodged in the flesh sparks out, leaping across
space into the the pearl of another's brain.

IV / BRISE MARINE

THREE UNKNOWN SEA CREATURES

1. Holothalma

Each curled, glaucous wave
Crashing against black rocks
Contains millions of us.
You've never seen us. You need
A thousand of us piled together
To make an illusory speck.
Hundreds of us once posed
On a microscope's slide,
Pretending to be a creature.
I played a stalky eye,
While friends piled themselves up,
Creating a segmented body,
Pearly, rainbow streaked,
Covered with nimble spines.
We received a Latin name
For the achievement of existence,
And celebrated for weeks,
Getting drunk on salt molecules
And teasing the sea cucumbers
Who tried to devour us.
You might hear us someday
As we gambol and breed,
But only if you're attentive,
For we speak in generations,
Harmonizing our shrieks
Just to make a faint hissing
Over the roar of the tide.

2. Glossoblastula

We're the sea-chameleons,
Able to disguise ourselves
As other hapless creatures,
Mutating our pliant bodies
Into the arms of that octopus
You're trying to spear,

Or shooting past you with fins
As you lean on the rail.
Of course it's just a deception,
For when you pull us on board
We're just some slimy stuff
Resembling glutinous seaweed,
So you throw us back
And we dive down and away,
Telling each other the story.
We do it just for fun,
Not to save our fellows
For we know they'd eat us, too,
If we were really shad,
Or baby flounder. Still,
We feel heroic at times,
And though we're often devoured
By humorless sharks,
We strut and gossip among
Sea anemone and starfish,
Glozing our errors,
And promising feats to come.

3. Podophedron

We live deep in the ocean
Grazing the abyssal plain,
Our thick, scaly bodies
Adapted to the cooling lava
Still seeping from a volcano
Whose hissing steam creates
Eden under the sea,
A jungle of swaying stems,
Giant grasses, and blossoms
Opening with bursts of bubbles.
We've grown gills down here
Since the Ice Age trapped us,
For unlike whales or dolphins,
We're too heavy to surface,
And prefer these dark depths,
Our long, ropy necks swinging

Back and forth in the weeds
As we nibble the brine varieties
Of palmettos and bananas,
Our massive, scalloped tails
Slapping up famous currents.
We lay one egg a century,
And feed our hatchlings
Masticated seaflowers,
Ignoring the voracious schools
That swim in and out of view,
Eating each other with joy.

BRISE MARINE

after Mallarmé

Nowadays my former students have grey hair
And sharpening lines around their somber eyes.
I expected to grow old. I'm used to it—
But to see the young aging is terrifying.
My flesh is sad. I've taught so many books
I want to run away to some far place
Where birds fly drunkenly above the foam.
Nothing, not even the tulips waiting to bloom,
Planted last fall under tumultuous clouds
In order to provide some natural hope,
Can hold back my heart, drenched in the sea.
As for these nights! Neither this desert of light
Cast by my study lamp, or this empty paper
Defending its white fibers against my pen,
Or my cat, Oleander, asleep on the divan,
Can stop me. I'm going to leave. Steamboat
Lift anchor for the exotic life down river
Where the Mississippi spills into the Gulf.

A Boredom, distilled by cruel delusions,
Still believes in the good-bye of handkerchiefs!
Though, perhaps, the tall decks, inviting hurricanes
As they glide slowly through the cotton fields
Toward New Orleans, and the sea-going masts,
Are those which a wind hastens over shipwrecks
Lost, without flags, without survivors
Or the unreachable islands of palm and banana. . .
But oh my heart, hear the song of the sirens.

STARFISH

I put my mind into a glass bottle
And let it drift out on the deadly sea
While a part-time ranger in high rubber boots
Spoke to us in kindergarten terms
About the life in tidepools—anemone, sea urchins.
She was going to show us the best pools, but first
Quizzed us to make us humble and ashamed
Of how little we knew of diatoms and kelp.
I longed to run ahead of the group, and pass
Through the tall arch of black, slippery rock
Where the cliff met the tide—where starfish lived.
Instead I watched the waves, as high as houses,
Lifting and falling through the pearly fog.
But then the ranger drew three linked circles
In the wet sand with a piece of driftwood
And ordered us to step into her tidepool—
We could be chitons, or barnacles, or clams.
I watched the adults shuffling into place,
Embarrassed but polite, while eager children
Opened their hungry mouths to eat their prey.
I stood on the edge, hoping to be ignored,
But soon she looked at me. She wasn't smiling.
She told me to choose a pool so she could start
Her illustrated lecture on the sea.
I laughed, then ran. Soon I was out of breath,
Clambering over the rocks in the fog
Until the arch grew larger and larger
And I passed through it to another beach
Empty and wild. Here brilliant sea life
Flowered in the shallow pools. I knelt
To watch the pulsing creatures, spiny green
Or rosy red, undulating and gleaming.
I couldn't name them or describe habits.
I knew they had hidden mouths, sex organs,
Ways of eating one another for survival—
But which was which? I'd chosen ignorance.
I saw the group I'd left come through the arch

And stand around a tide pool for the talk
That would explain, and clarify, and name.
Swiftly I kept going. The beach narrowed.
A tall cliff rose beside the sea, and high
Above my head I saw the foamy line
That marked high tide. I had no charts
Or knowledge of the sea booming before me.
Suddenly I found a clinging starfish
Beneath a rock, as large as a day lily—
A starfish from a dream, alive and soft.
I knelt on the wet sand, memorizing
The shape and texture, finding the eye,
Or something like an eye. I saw it quiver,
Then had to jump away as a wave rolled in
And covered up the rock in creamy foam.
When I looked again, the starfish was gone,
Dragged back to sea where I imagined it
Spinning down to some hidden cavern
Where a thousand starfish glowed on the walls,
More stars than fish, and every one my own.

SEA CASTLE

In grammar school we all had jobs
To teach us what real life was like:
Some of us had to pound erasers,
Or scrub desktops with paper towels;
I had to wipe the cloakroom floor
With a sour-smelling mop
That looked like grey, witch's hair.
The best job was feeding the fish
In the new, donated aquarium.
I envied the girl who sprinkled flecks
Across the surface of the water
Calling the fish out of their castle
To graze and shimmer
Above the graceful, living gardens
Of anemone and seaweed.
One day, putting away my mop,
I walked close to the aquarium.
I saw the fish staring out
Through the glass walls of the tank,
Looking at the restless feet
And tender necks of thirty children.
Suddenly I was among the fish:
I felt the soft slap of water,
The armor of my gleaming scales.
I leapt ahead toward the ramparts
Of the great towering castle,
Flashing and somersaulting,
Surprising the experienced fish,
Who looked with cool, ironical eyes
As I entered the coral arch—
For inside the rooms were plain,
The water grey and shadowy.
Two dull-colored fish swam by me
Opening their mouths to let out bubbles
So beautiful I trembled;
But when I tried to talk to them
None of us could make a sound.

Quickly the fish swam away
And I moved on through empty vaults
Trying to find a gorgeous chamber,
Lined with mother of pearl or mosaics,
Where all the ancient treasure was stored,
Greek wine-cups, and jeweled swords
From Elizabethan scabbards—
But the endless rooms grew darker
Until I reached a stagnant dungeon.
Soon I felt, rather than saw,
Dim, uncertain shapes
Twisting past me in the murk.
Abruptly I came upon
A writhing fish, my own size,
Being eaten alive by sea snakes
Undulating as they fed
Greedily on its heart and brain.
Seeing me, the snakes quivered
And tried to fasten their mouths
On my raised dorsal fin.
Gasping, I shot away in horror
And swam back out
Into the clear, open water
Where now a golden feather dangled
Before the wary eyes of the fish
Who kept far from its dancing spin,
Knowing that it hid a hook.
I meant to bite it, and return
Safely to my familiar desk
But first pressed my cold-blooded face
Against the thick wall of glass
To see what the fish dreaded—
I saw my classmate's grown-up lives:
Tommy in his pressed suit,
An undertaker like his father,
And Joan typing with red nails
To feed her alcoholic mother;
Roger carrying a black pail
To work the line at Caterpillar.
I shivered, and then saw myself

Washing an iron roasting pan,
My hair set in tiny pincurls.
I wore a blue maternity dress
And yellow Latex rubber gloves;
My diamond ring was glittering
On the counter by the Brillo pad.
But I'd never live a life like that!
I felt a throbbing in my gills,
Knowing I had to go back down
And roam the hushed, gloomy halls
Of the treacherous sea castle
All by myself,
Or else bite the gleaming hook
Ready to pull me up on land
Where the adults waited with knives.

DEN LILLE HAVFRUE

Andersen's forlorn mermaid sits
On her wave-lashed rock in the bay.
She's cast in bronze and soldered down,
Her half-formed feet just visible
Through the viscous web of fish scale
Resolving into a pair of legs.

She looks exactly as I dreamed.
I used to read "The Little Mermaid"
When I was sick and couldn't walk
I loved her underwater kingdom
Protected by a sky of waves
Where fish sang in the red trees,

And later, when I ran and leapt,
An ordinary child of eight,
I longed to see the far off world
She chose when she accepted pain—
Scented flowers, snowy mountains,
The prince on his marble balcony.

Now, across the bay, oil tankers
Nudge ashore with their rich cargo.
The tall refinery smokestacks
Pierce the blustery horizon,
And nobody calculates the depth
Of the sea with church steeples.

Head averted from us mortals,
The Little Mermaid seems to sigh.
Our earth is smaller than she thought,
Our souls as vaporous as foam.
What ocean is this, reclaiming her,
Painting her breasts and thighs with scum?

LABYRINTH

Each word's a stone, a paving stone, a flat rock, and like the little girl who trod on a loaf to save herself in the swamp but still sank down until she was grasped by the Marsh King, I step on the word blue, a color, and feel myself descending slowly to the labyrinth below, the mind-swamp. Blue wobbles under my feet, the color of my school uniform, going deeper now, blue the color of the outer garment the Virgin Mary wore over her white smock on the altar. I'm already waist deep in blue, the waves slosh up around my breasts, small waves, this is the blue chlorine of the swimming pool, the boys grabbing my ankles as I kick away from the side, my blue strap sliding down, he's seen my nipple, shriveled and blue. Now I'm up to my neck, the weight of my step still pushing blue deeper into the murk, but as the sludge covers my eyes I find not darkness but a blue phosphorescence, I can see through this medium, everything shining and strange, distorted. Isn't that flower the earring I lost in Alaska? Aren't those snakes really the suede boots I pulled up against my calves that year I wore the mini-skirt and kissed too many mouths, my heart filled with shaved ice? And aren't those dim stars the Mexican glasses I loved, resurrected from their broken fragments? Blue sinks and sinks. I see tunnels branching off. Other words float past at different levels, suspended and buoyant, some of them hard and shiny with mica, others porous like sponges. I reach out for one, but my fingers slip away, I'm traveling faster on blue, the weight of my body forcing it down below all the others, but how far down, is there a Minotaur who waits to thrust up out of the dimness with gaping jaws to show me I know nothing about blue, or will I at last reach the sand at the bottom where fish sing among the branching coral, and my dead father's eyes look mildly at me from a dolphin's body?

NOCTURNE AFTER MIDNIGHT

"I want to appear a success even to myself."
—Virginia Woolf

Superstitious? I believe in nothing.
And yet, look at this unfinished painting.
How many times I've rubbed this figure out
As it struggles to emerge into the light.
A dash of paint—there—it's gone again.
I'm after gleams and tones, not phantom form
Thrusting up through color—a seal? a mermaid?
A drowned sailor?—trying to tell the story
My brush conceals with every stroke, as if
I had to tell it. Look at my hands.
You've watched me snatching food, you've wondered
Why I slip crackers and pieces of ham
Compulsively into my pockets. Once a friend
Saw me wrap a roll in a dinner napkin,
And leaned across the table. "You're rich, now.
Why do you save scraps from restaurant lunches?"
I flushed. "In case I get hungry later."
What other reason, I thought. But that night,
Rummaging through the jumble of my bag,
I found five bundles of disgusting food,
Stale bread, moldy cheese, two bitten doughnuts.
Opening my refrigerator, I saw doggy bags
Stacked on the back shelves, shriveled pizza,
Chinese noodles from a gallery opening,
And I raged at myself.

                    Once, years ago,
When I was penniless, but afraid of debt,
Skipping meals to buy my canvases,
I painted the portraits of three young girls
Whose parents insisted I live at their house,
Taking meals with the family, and using
A long, covered veranda as my studio.
The sea became the background for the paintings,
Though the light changed for each sitting,

Dawn light for Gemma, the oldest, who rose
Obediently at five every morning
So I could get that shade of blue and mauve
Behind her, the purple streaks on the water.
I liked the shadowy hollows of her cheeks,
Her fine, thin bones. She always sat so still,
Her hands resting in her lap, a half-smile
Pleated onto her face as if she were already
A painting, and I was copying a master.
Next Beatrice arrived. I captured
Sunny pleasantness, her straight eye-brows,
That look she had of trying hard to stifle
A yawn. After lunch I worked on Frannie,
The youngest, who couldn't keep still.
I arranged her holding her little terrier
Until he squirmed and barked, trying to get
Her sense of continual motion into paint.

But all day long I dreaded the dinner hour.
I'd clean my stained hands, and wash away
My confidence with the lavender soap,
Arriving at the table out of breath,
My throat clenched so tight I couldn't speak
Except in whispers. What was wrong with me?
I felt exposed and humble, like a fly
Buzzing around the rim of a sugar bowl,
Drunk on the heavenly scents, but aware
That any moment I'd be swatted down
For my pretensions. Oh, I can't explain.
Maybe it was just those noisy mealtimes
When I was a kid, all of us crowded
Onto benches, slurping our chocolate milk,
Elbowing each other, stuffing our mouths
As the TV blared from the top of the fridge,
And neighbor kids pressed their noses flat
To the screen door, yelling for us to hurry.
I learned to eat fast as my brothers reached
For more across my plate, my stomach tense
And cramping as I eyed the extra piece
Of bread, meant for the one who finished first.

My cheeks puffed as I gobbled and chewed
Meat-loaf, fish sticks, or pigs-in-a-blanket.
When the squabbling got too loud, our father
Shouted for us all to shut our traps,
While our mother only sighed, too busy
Even to eat as she mopped up our spills,
And fed strained carrots to the fussy baby.

I'd always dreamed of dining like my patrons—
Cocktails on silver trays for the adults,
Pink linen, crystal, heavy pewter bowls,
Platters of tiny fowl in delicate sauces,
Hard-crusted rolls, braised vegetables,
And candles winking in the French windows
As the sun dropped like a peach into the sea.
Such abundance. The rolls, glazed with egg,
Gleamed in the basket. I reached for one,
Then drew back my hand in embarrassment,
Afraid to reveal my bad manners or my hunger,
Confusing the two, perhaps. My face tingled
And grew numb. I felt as if everyone
Around the table was watching my fork,
Waiting for something to drip or splatter,
And I couldn't swallow what I longed to gulp.
But Gemma noticed my gesture. Her eyes
Met mine. She handed me her uneaten roll
Under cover of the table cloth. I took it,
Slipped it quickly into my shirt pocket,
And felt the muscles unknit in my neck,
Knowing I could gnaw and chew it later
Unobserved behind the locked door of my room.
And after that it happened every meal.
Gemma slipped me the things she didn't eat
Off her plate, under the cover of talk—
Her father describing his partner's tennis serve,
Her mother recalling a cruise to Bermuda.

Why didn't I notice that Gemma was ill?
I was thin myself, my ribs and pelvis
Visible through my skin. It seemed normal.

I accepted her roast beef, her red pears,
Her untouched sandwiches at lunch, saving
Everything she gave me in my room
Where I'd nibble tiny bites, or just smell
The winey odors, my fear of hunger
Appeased, though not my hunger. I knew
That if I ate the food, I'd have none left
For later, and I hoarded all I could,
So that I'd be able to give the illusion
Of fitting small bites of coq au vin
Into my mouth in public without shame.
And so the long summer slowly unfolded.
My favorite time was dawn, painting Gemma,
Her rope of black hair over one shoulder,

The sound of the sea not yet diminished
By all the traffic on the road above us.
After a while I hardly looked at her
As I defined the sea, scumbled the clouds,
Harmonizing the light with my vision
While she confided things in a soft voice.
She told me she longed to be a cellist
But now, after five years of lessons,
She knew she wasn't good enough. I tried
To reassure her, told her it was all desire
And practice, but she sighed and shrugged,
As if she'd heard that dangerous undertone
I had to fight against in my own head,
A rushing tide of voices whispering
That I was wrong to think I was a genius.
I remember how at an early stage
I'd sketched her in outline so that the sea,
Shone visibly as streaks of Thalo Blue
Right through her body, not yet repainted,
And when she stepped up to see my work,
She said she saw herself that way in dreams.

I got two notes in Christmas cards from Gemma.
The first I answered. The second reached me
Only months later, forwarded to my new address

In Provincetown, and I remember placing it
With a stack of other notes, meaning to answer—
But life whirled ahead, and Gemma dropped
Into the growing pool of people I'd forgotten
Along with my early, commissioned paintings
That now seem so romantic and allusive.
Then, for my retrospective at the Whitney,
Her family loaned their now valuable portraits,
And, shocked, I learned that Gemma had died
At twenty-two, a music student, weighing
Hardly more than her own priceless cello.
Frannie told me the facts, how they'd smashed
The lock of her Brooklyn Heights studio
To find her on the bed like a skeleton,
Her shelves crowded with gift boxes of jams,
Caviar, and fancy chocolates her parents
Had mailed her every week from the best stores.
That night at the opening, I kept drifting
Among acquaintances, shaking hands, hugging,
But my throat ached. I didn't feel triumphant.
I kept coming back to that spot on the wall,
Gemma's mouth a dark slash, the eyes staring
Straight ahead, sea-colored, seductive,
Knowing I'd helped destroy what I created.

Sometimes at night I go look at the sea,
Watching ruffs of foam sweep up the shore
As if the moon had brushed them on the water,
And when I come back, I paint from memory.
Here's the palette of my inner world,
Cobalt, Viridian, Mars Black—
But knowing how I'm made, what shades mix
With what shadows, only makes me doubt
The neutrality of this strange figure
Clawing to the surface of my canvas.
The more I paint it out, the more it tries
To break through the nocturnal tones and washes
Of my abstraction. There's that hand again,
Just where the paint is thick and swirling.
Do you see it? Must I paint it, then,

86

Give it a sex and a name? Call it Gemma,
Or some ancient image of myself, rising up
Like a sea-creature, writhing and thrashing,
Head sleek above the waves as it attacks?